THE TATTOO COLOURING BOOK

MEGAMUNDEN

LAURENCE KING PUBLISHING

Published in 2013 by
LAURENCE KING PUBLISHING LTD
361-373 City Road
London EC1V 1LR
Tel. +4420 7841 6900
Fax. +4420 7841 6910
e-mail:enquiries@laurenceking.com
www.laurenceking.com

Reprinted 2013, 2014 (three times), 2015 (twice)

~

DESIGN BY: JOHNNY MCCULLOCH

~

A catalogue record for this book is available
from The British Library.

ISBN-978-1-78067-0-126
PRINTED IN CHINA

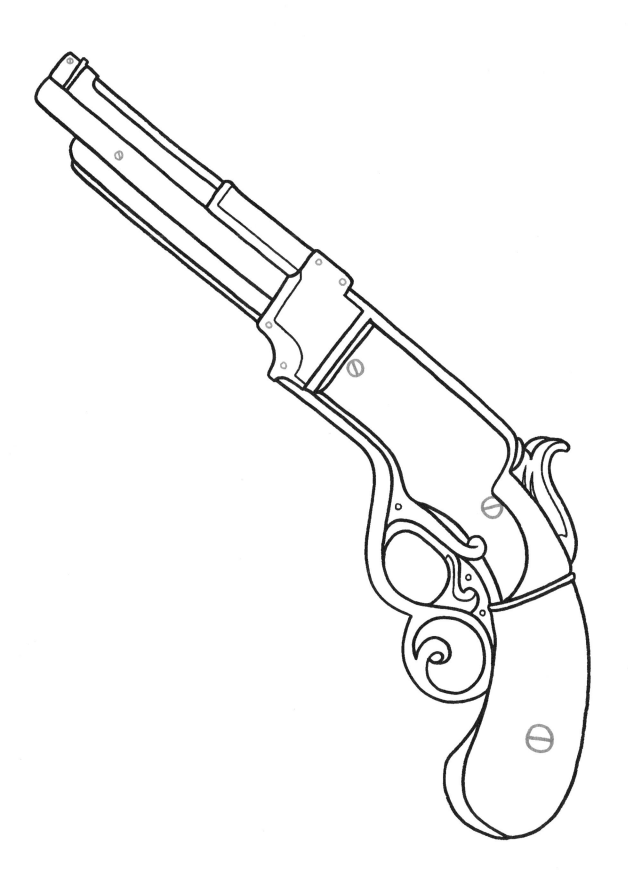

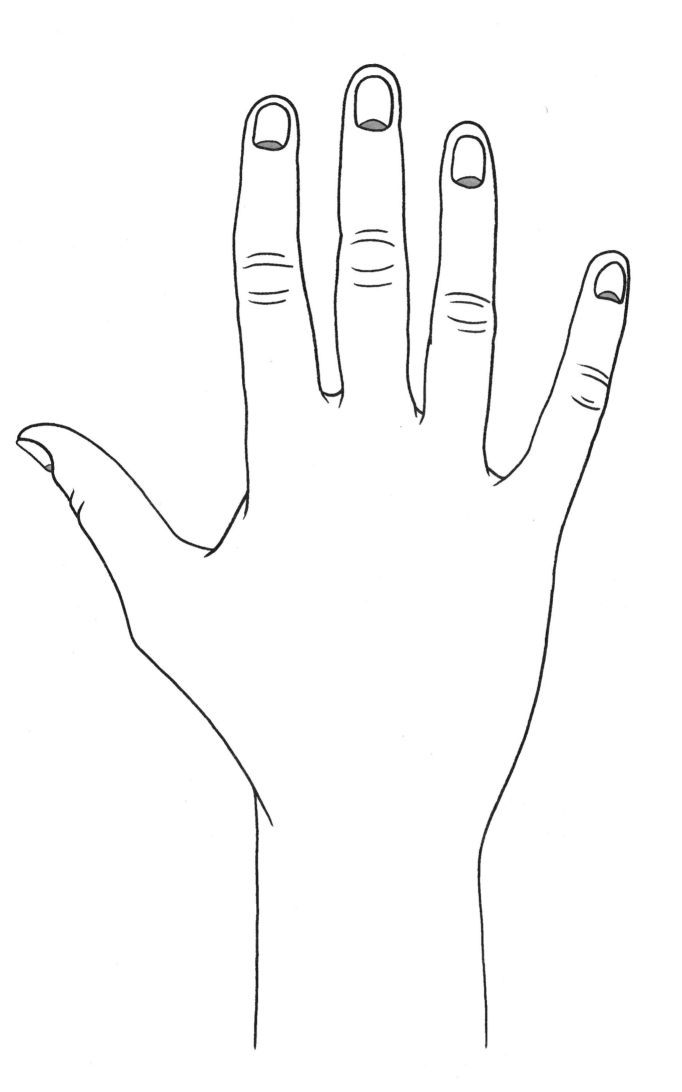

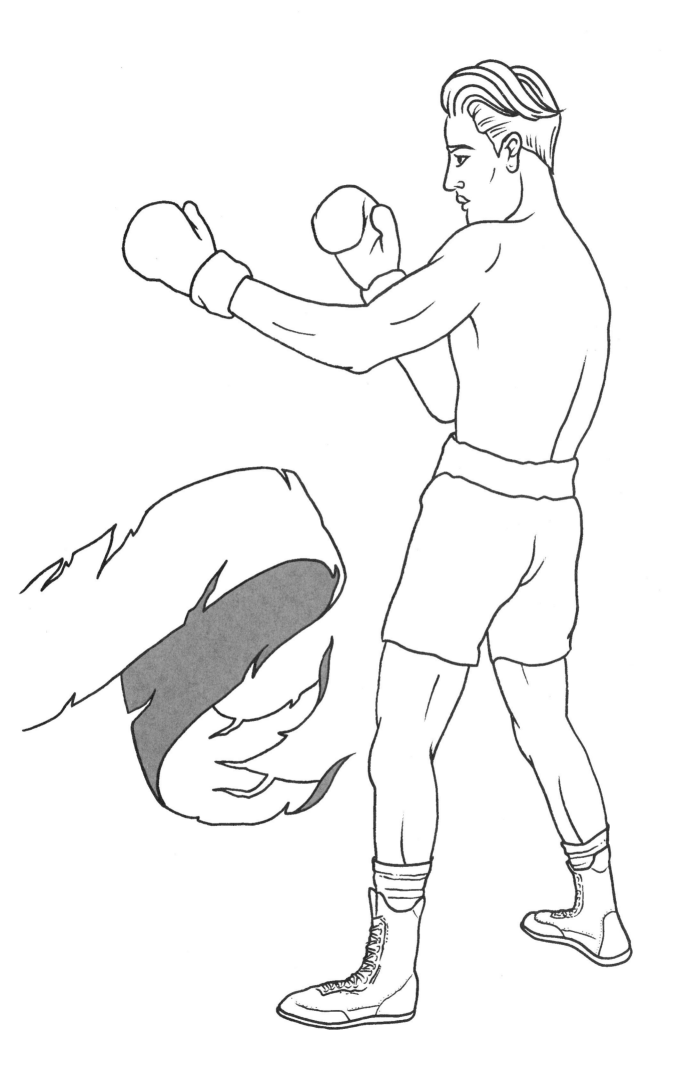

I'd like to say a huge thank you to everyone that helped, encouraged and tolerated me during the creation of this book... it's been a long road.

Special thanks go to Vanessa, David & Joshua Munden, Stephanie Iles, Neil Davies, Ben Griffin, Mark Graham and Ben Beach along with everyone at Ilovedust...

...and lastly but most importantly a MEGA thank you goes to Johnny McCulloch. Without his ideas, motivational speaking and general all-round support this book would have never come to fruition.

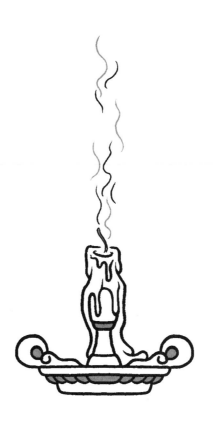